Small Spaces and Cozy Corners

COUNTRY LIVING
EASY TRANSFORMATIONS

Small Spaces and Cozy Corners

Janice Easton-Epner

HEARST BOOKS
A Division of Sterling Publishing Co., Inc.
New York

A Primrose Productions Book
Designed by Stephanie Stislow

Library of Congress Cataloging-in-Publication Data
Easton-Epner, Janice.
  Country living easy transformations : small spaces and cozy corners / Janice Easton-Epner.
       p. cm.
  Includes index.
  ISBN 1-58816-427-6
  1. Small rooms--Decoration. 2. Interior decoration--Human factors.
  I. Title: Easy transformations. II. Country living. III. Title.

  NK2117.S59E2 2005
  747--dc22

                                                                2004018282

    10   9   8   7   6   5   4   3   2   1

Published by Hearst Books
A Division of Sterling Publishing Co., Inc.
387 Park Avenue South, New York, NY 10016

Country Living is a trademark owned by Hearst Magazines Property, Inc., in USA, and Hearst Communications, Inc., in Canada. Hearst Books is a trademark owned by Hearst Communications, Inc.

www.countryliving.com

Distributed in Canada by Sterling Publishing
℅ Canadian Manda Group, 165 Dufferin Street
Toronto, Ontario, Canada M6K 3H6

Distributed in Australia by Capricorn Link (Australia) Pty. Ltd.
P.O. Box 704, Windsor, NSW 2756 Australia

Manufactured in China

ISBN 1-58816-427-6

Contents

A B O V E : This small hallway has many elements that make it work. First, the boldly striped rugs lead the eye up the staircase and echo the clapboard ceiling. Next, the wonderful wooden artwork on the walls breaks up all those straight lines with its circular forms. Finishing touches include the chair, flowers, and, of course, the charming cocker spaniel.

Foreword

There's an old saying, "Good things come in small packages." It's the same with decorating: Sometimes the most creative ideas are found in the coziest spots. After all, spacious living rooms, dining rooms, kitchens, and bedrooms have plenty of elbowroom to play with the placement of furniture and accessories. Imbuing a foyer, landing, hallway, or tiny nook with personality and charm is more of a challenge.

Small Spaces and Cozy Corners meets this challenge head on. Throughout the book you'll find lots of great ideas. Some suggestions are as simple as hanging an eye-catching work of art on the wall or placing a graphic hooked rug underfoot. Others involve arranging a few favorite objects on a windowsill or positioning a comfy club chair in an otherwise unassuming corner. Success may require finding new uses for old things, like having an antique garden ladder serve as an attractive bookshelf.

Best of all, each of the options presented here takes into consideration the constraints on time and budget that we all face today. Whether you are just beginning to decorate your home or are simply looking for a few finishing touches, inspiration awaits you on the pages ahead.

Nancy Mernit Soriano
Editor-in-Chief
Country Living

ABOVE : This collection of pitchers and vases is much stronger when grouped together than when spread throughout the home. In this arrangement, you can appreciate each one in relation to the others and note the differences in colors, glazes, and slight variations in style.

Introduction

Most people decorate their homes by focusing on one room at a time, neglecting the tricky corners, long hallways, stairway landings, or other odd spaces that present difficulties. *Small Spaces and Cozy Corners* tackles these areas directly, presenting dozens of design solutions and creative ideas to help you make the most of awkward spaces. With the help of judicious decorative touches, problem areas can be fully integrated into your home's design, and may even become one of your favorite places to linger.

Although it may seem contrary to conventional wisdom, small, neglected spaces can actually set the design tone for the entire home. In large spaces, such as a living room, a design scheme gets spread out, and occasionally even diluted or lost. In small areas, however, a strong statement about your home's design theme conveys the message clearly, and can lead one to see other rooms in a new light.

Don't let the challenge of small or awkward spaces intimidate you. Allow your creativity full reign; you will often find that your first impulse is the best one to follow. If a vintage piece strikes your fancy at a local flea market, by all means, snatch it up. Decorating a space does not mean following someone else's rigid formula; rather, it is the refining of your personal choices to make visual sense and add clarity. The design principles offered here are not hard and fast rules, and each space is unique—only you can decide what works best in your own home.

Our intention in *Small Spaces and Cozy Corners* is to aid you in charting your own course by presenting creative ideas, design solutions, and handy tips for you to follow. Some of these ideas are as easy as learning how to vary the sizes and heights of objects in order to add visual interest to a display, or how to create a focal point with color. Other ideas are intended to free you from old design tenets and bring fresh air into your décor, like mixing formal and informal elements or adding unusual pieces. Along the way, we provide specific solutions for small spaces, like storage or seating, and advice for repeating colors and themes strategically, along with tips and simple projects to get you started.

Welcoming in Style

The title of this chapter has a dual meaning. First, it is meant as encouragement for you to let the doors open wide and welcome style into your home—particularly into those small spaces, odd nooks, and cozy corners that might otherwise be ignored. Second, in rethinking the decoration in those spaces, the best way to begin is to imagine them from the perspective of guests entering your home: how would you like to welcome them and make them feel at ease?

Start outside, by walking up the steps or porch, and entering the vestibule, foyer, or entryway. Study the area from every angle. This space greets anyone visiting your home—you want it to be more than a dropping ground for mail, backpacks, groceries, or coats. Remember that old expression about first impressions? If your entry area is neglected and bare, or cluttered and cramped, your carefully designed living room will have a lot of compensating to do. On the other hand, you can decorate entrances—no matter how small or awkwardly shaped—with complementary colors, fabrics, or furniture that reflect the themes of the main rooms of your home, thereby greeting your guests with the warm comfort of your personal style.

L E F T : From the billowing American flag outside to the rag rug and handwoven basket on the rough-hewn bench, this entry is not only welcoming and attractive, but also leads the guest to expect a home decorated in the Early American style.

ABOVE: If your décor is Early American or Colonial, choose period–appropriate details to make a front hallway more than a passage to the main rooms. Here, a ladder-back chair, dried flowers, and a decorative arrangement of homespun fabric hung on wooden pegs gives the hallway its own charm.

LEFT: The gentle curves of the wooden table and chair temper the rigid architectural lines of this corner. A container of dried hydrangeas and a botanical print on the wall serve to finish the space and connect it to the garden beyond.

RIGHT: If you are lucky enough to have an old Victorian home with a wraparound porch, why not add a few decorative touches to link the exterior and interior? Here, a wrought-iron daybed dressed in antique linens evokes the hospitality of an earlier era, as do the added touches of pillows and flowers, more of which are to be found inside.

A CHANDELIER IN THE FOYER? WHY NOT? BREAKING WITH THE EXPECTED LEADS TO TRULY CREATIVE DECORATING.

LEFT: This foyer is brassy, eccentric and fun. The owner's passions— a love of flea market finds and of Texas (witness the bold star on the front door) are telegraphed to all who enter. The addition of the mirror directly across from the front door is a stroke of wit—what could be more welcoming than seeing your own face upon entering?

L E F T : An entrance that opens directly onto a stairway doesn't have to be a detriment. The interior design of this foyer incorporates the stairway as an element of design: the crossed lines of the chair back make the diagonal line of the staircase more dramatic, and the photographs of flowers are positioned to correspond with the stair risers.

THE CURVES OF THE CIRCULAR LIGHT FIXTURE COUNTER ALL THE ANGULARITY IN THE FOYER.

A B O V E : This porch becomes an outdoor living space with a wooden lounge featuring a storage trundle. The charming pressed-tin mail basket adds just the right touch—at once decorative and hardworking.

LEFT: When the season or the occasion demands, change the theme on your porch—a brief transformation gives any home a quick lift. This Halloween doorway has just the right combination of spooky lighting, autumnal leaves, and vintage black-and-orange paper decorations to be sinister and eerily welcoming at the same time.

ABOVE: For those with a green thumb, the decorative possibilities include a whole world of plants. On this L-shaped porch, English roses and exuberant greenery transform the space into a cheerful extension of the garden.

A B O V E : For those of you with only a step between front door and dining area—a common enough situation for apartment dwellers—even a basket of flowers can help define the entry. Here, a bare wooden floor in the entryway gives way to a warmer feeling in the dining room created by an area rug placed under the table.

A B O V E : A clean and spare porch with just a bench or chair can be easily transformed with just a few appropriate accessories kept nearby for special occasions. These plaid cotton-rayon throws can be stored conveniently in a front closet and are not only pretty but also practical, creating a spot to sit comfortably outdoors.

Easy Transformation Tip

Nothing says summertime relaxation like wicker. To keep your wicker furniture bright and cheery from year to year, clean it thoroughly at the beginning of the season. First, with a brush attachment, vacuum thoroughly to remove dust and dirt. Then, working outdoors, wash the wicker down with a garden hose while using a scrub brush and soap suds to loosen and remove any remaining dirt trapped inside the weave. Hose down liberally to rinse off the suds before letting the wicker dry completely. To restore old wicker, wash with warm water, air dry, and apply a thin layer of lacquer to protect the surface.

L E F T : One corner of a narrow porch becomes a favorite spot to lounge with the addition of a reclining chaise.

R I G H T : An all-weather statue like this is a great way to add personality to an entry. It takes up little space, requires virtually no maintenance, and lends a warm and comforting touch.

Themes and Collections

Some people hear the term "theme" and think, "Oh no, that's too planned or artificial for me." But a theme needn't feel like a program that has been followed in lockstep. Certainly, if you adore southwestern style or want to create the look of an 1880s prairie home in your living room, you can follow a fully executed theme. But a theme can also be simply the use of certain colors or the creation of a certain feeling. Corners offer excellent spots in which to focus your theme before spreading it throughout the room or home. Done well, any theme can be conveyed with subtlety—you want to express your interests, not present a museum exhibit.

A theme is an excellent way to incorporate personal collections, which can otherwise linger on the top shelves of closets or in boxes. After all, good decorating is not about slavishly following a formula; rather, it is meant to be a statement of personal taste or personality. Collections can also be a starting point for decorative inspiration: design your home around the colors or textures of the objects you love, and you're sure to be pleased with the result. Away from the flow of everyday traffic, corners offer wonderful areas to display collections to their fullest, and these displays can really show off a theme or color scheme.

LEFT: This simple yet elegant corner is a wonderful example of how to get an Early American flavor without spending money on expensive historical or reproduction pieces. A folksy table is paired with a vintage-style splint basket, and a cast-iron urn from the early 1900s plays home to a delightfully exuberant plant.

ABOVE: Grouped in a glass-fronted cabinet, this collection of vintage vases sets the tone for the room. A wonderful floral display of peonies and seashells offers a study in contrasting textures and natural forms.

ABOVE: Consider the tabletop as an invitation to create a vignette—an eye- or light-catching juxtaposition of textures and shapes. Here, surrounded by the botanicals and bell jars, a windmill suggests a poignant tale.

RIGHT: In this softly feminine corner, the potential difficulties posed by an irregular wall interrupted by a window and a doorway that shortens the connecting wall have been turned to the collector's advantage. A comfy chair slipcovered in white anchors a corner in which a garden theme is expressed through a variety of floral collectibles mixed with live blooms. The distressed finish of the mantel keep the space from being too precious; instead, it is pretty and welcoming.

ABOVE: This windowed corner becomes a perfect display area for old milk bottles paired with a casual arrangement of lilacs. Wicker was a wise choice here, echoing the slats of the full-length interior shutters.

A COLUMN OF SIMPLE, CUSTOM SHELVES GRADUATING IN SIZE TRANSFORMS THIS AWKWARD CORNER INTO A SMALL BUT PERFECT DISPLAY AREA FOR A BELOVED COLLECTION OF VINTAGE VASES.

ABOVE: When a dining room is not in use, a large, empty table seems forlorn. Use it to display the season's bounty; here, a free-form arrangement of vases holds a sampling of nature's offerings.

ABOVE: A corner bordered by floor-to-ceiling windows is warmed up by a table and chair in contrasting patterns. Earth-toned McCoy pottery, complemented by an alabaster bowl filled with shellacked dried eggs, link the interior to the landscape outdoors.

THE URN-LIKE SHAPE OF THE LAMP BASE MAKES IT A GOOD CHOICE NEXT TO THE SIMILARLY SHAPED POTTERY.

RIGHT: A small nook is an opportunity—in this case, to create a work space that is accessible but not in the way of the main flow of activity in the room.

ABOVE: Feel free to break the "rules" of display. These shadow boxes, casually jumbled in a corner, are far more evocative and playful than if they were positioned regimentally to cover the wall.

IF YOU MAKE YOURSELF A HOBBY CORNER, KEEP THE CLUTTER UNDER CONTROL WITH DECORATIVE STORAGE. HERE, MATERIALS ARE GROUPED ATTRACTIVELY IN VINTAGE CONTAINERS SO THAT THEY BECOME A FOCAL POINT INSTEAD OF AN EYESORE.

L E F T : Open shelves are great for pieces of different sizes, like this milk glass. The sometimes unused spaces between windows or above radiators are excellent spots for shelving.

A B O V E : A flea-market hutch with a chicken-wire front fits nicely here, perfect for displaying a collection of colorful blue vases.

L E F T : Corners were made for cupboards like this one. Filling it with a single collection makes a dramatic statement. Displaying some of the marbled vases on their sides highlights the sculptural quality of their design.

DON'T FORGET THE TOPS OF CABINETS: THEY OFFER DISPLAY SPACE THAT IS VISIBLE BUT NOT TOUCHABLE.

ABOVE: Restrained arrangements give a rhythmic structure to these collections so that they enhance the room instead of overpowering it.

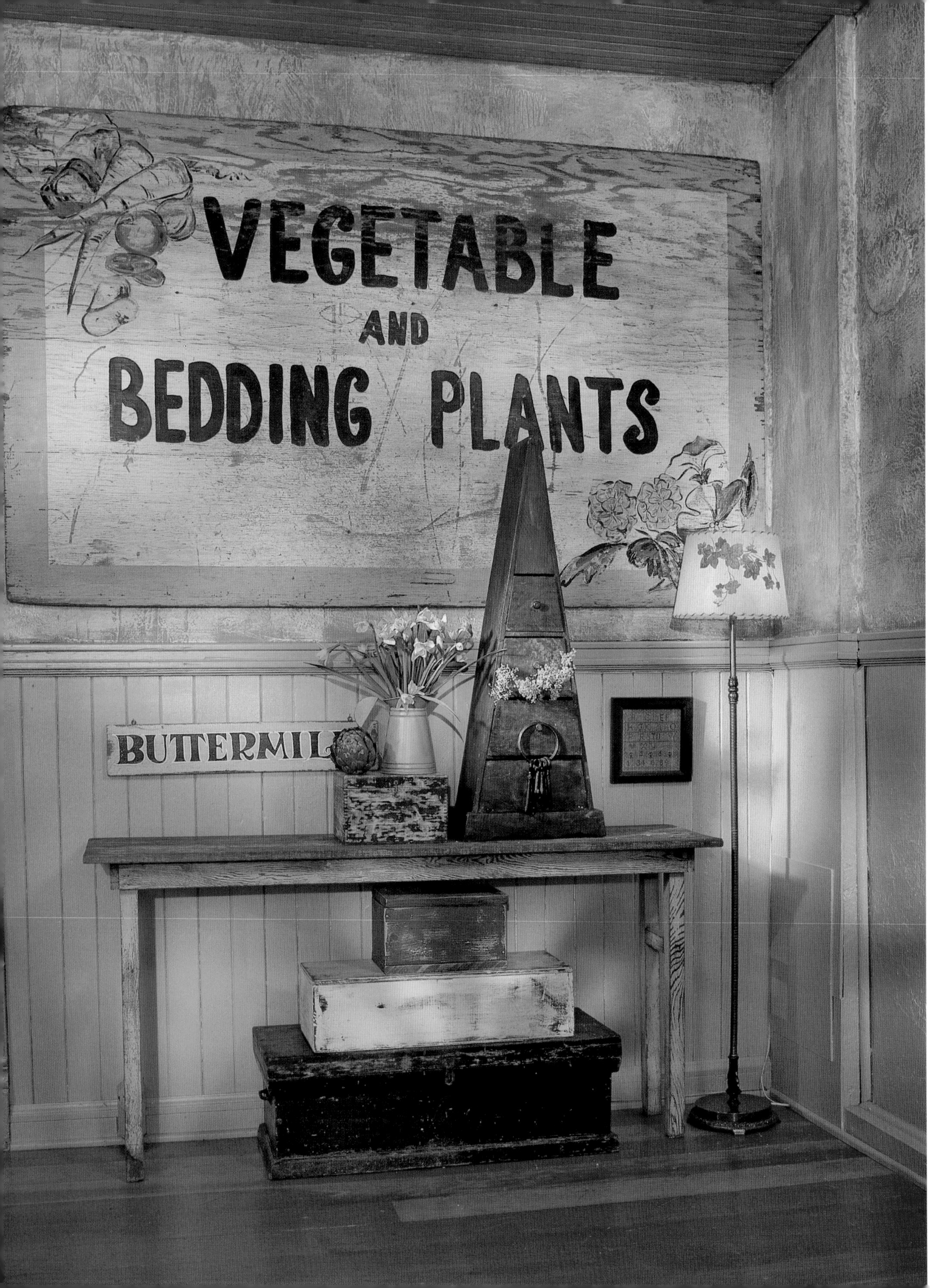
VEGETABLE
AND
BEDDING PLANTS
BUTTERMIL

LEFT: This corner display is a study in good placement. Note how the triangular chest is set just below the 'A' in "plants," and the table display sits directly above the stacked boxes, which add support to the entire grouping.

ABOVE: An otherwise unused corner is home to two collections—a stack of country benches and a group of yellow McCoy vases. Filling just one or two of the vases with flowers provides a reminder that they have a purpose beyond just looking pretty.

A B O V E : On a narrow strip of wall, shadow boxes display and protect a collection. Each piece of silver is a decorative object all its own: the serving spoon, Bakelite-handled fork, and man's clothes brush recall an earlier time.

R I G H T : A rustic cabinet calls for a more dramatic display. Majolica is beautiful enough that it is tempting to put out only a single piece, but this grouping yields a more impressive result, and is a nice complement to the massive wooden cabinet.

Connecting Spaces

Staircases, hallways, and doorways are among the most neglected and ignored spaces in any house, and few design books offer suggestions for these hardworking areas. These spaces are all connectors, that is, links between the different rooms of a house. Corridors, stairways, and doors all connect rooms that may feature different designs, themes, and colors, not to mention functions. Therefore, decorating these areas can be fairly tricky, with the result that many homeowners try to play down their importance. Resist! With a little creativity and verve, you can make these forgotten spaces wonderful areas in themselves as well as appealing passages to the rooms beyond.

Because these are such functional areas, many people think of them as requiring no decoration whatsoever, other than maybe some carpet. Even the shortest staircase, hallway, or doorway, however, deserves some embellishment. One approach is to use a connecting space to help tie together the décor of your house. Another is to allow it to be appreciated by itself, especially if it can provide a home for some other loved but possibly neglected objects. The elements to consider are lighting, color, texture, and your overall theme.

LEFT: Stark and functional, this staircase mirrors the architecture of the home. Unsoftened by the usual drapery, the window stands out on its own, its trim framing the view beyond. The light shining in gives the old apothecary jars—the sole decoration—a lovely glow.

LEFT: The staircase is a perfect place to display holiday decorations, adding a festive feeling to an otherwise unnoticed area. A simple confection of garlands and tulle can be wrapped around the posts, here adding to the Victorian style of the tabletop display.

ABOVE: Winter garlands of white pine draped over rungs and gathered by ribbon add a soft, undulating quality to this usually stark staircase while providing a fragrant reminder of the season.

A B O V E : A stairwell is a particularly good spot to put up a family gallery—the images are easily viewable but cannot overpower the décor. Place photographs in an attractive pattern, and the stairwell becomes a much more entertaining place to linger.

L E F T : Climbing or descending the stairs in this rustic log cabin, one comes across a portrait of Abraham Lincoln. In a living room, it might convey a museum feel; in a bedroom, an incongruous lack of intimacy—but it's perfect in the stairway.

LEFT: In a room with a cathedral ceiling, the second-floor hallway often becomes part of the room below. This can be challenging for amateur decorators, but here is an excellent solution. A tall, narrow piece of art, difficult to place in most spaces, fits perfectly here, linking the upper corridor with the living room zone and drawing the eye upward.

A MULTICOLORED RUG CAN BE USED TO LINK THE PALETTE OF ONE ROOM TO THE NEXT.

ABOVE: A hooked rug is a wonderful decoration for a staircase and offers some traction on a potentially slippery surface. This bold geometric pattern adds visual excitement to the ascent.

Easy Transformation Tip

When you have a lovely old staircase like this, no additional ornamentation is necessary. It is important, however, to maintain the quality and luster of the wood. If your wood becomes stained, here are several stain removal techniques you can try to maintain the wood's uniform look:

• Scour the stains with a towel dipped in mineral spirits (wear rubber gloves).

• If that doesn't work, try a mix of equal parts vinegar and linseed oil.

• Still no luck? Then fit a hand sander with medium-grit sandpaper and lightly sand the dark spots; if sanding gets rid of the stains, you can refinish the sanded areas to match the balance of the flooring.

• If the stains are still there, you have a hard decision to make: You can either live with them, or refinish the entire staircase. Replacing the blemished boards might not solve your problem because the new wood might not match the old boards' color and wear.

RIGHT: What to do with a small nook beneath a curved stairwell? In this serenely elegant space, a slipcovered chair introduces a softer element (and a place to sit), while a photograph placed off-center behind it adds a note of visual excitement. The result might be considered a micro-gallery.

RIGHT: A landing on a stair-case should not be a dumping ground for clutter: take back that space with a striking piece of furniture. Both practical and beautiful, this old pie cupboard has taken on new life as a home for an antique quilt collection. The pitcher and water basin both top off the effect visually.

IF YOU'RE REALLY SHORT ON SPACE, AND YOU DON'T NEED THE LIGHT, DON'T BE AFRAID TO BLOCK OR PARTIALLY COVER A WINDOW.

ABOVE: The clear, clean lines of Colonial craftsmanship provide this staircase with its own visual appeal, making an attractive runner the only necessary accessory. In the narrow hallway below, a bench relieves the stark simplicity and offers a spot to rest.

LEFT: This staircase is fully decked out, and the effect is electrifying. Black-and-white vintage photographs are arranged cleverly on the wall starting about knee-high and inching forward by a foot every two steps. The stair runner adds vertical lines, and the white molding contrasts with the painted wall. Decorative doodads centered on the side of each stair provide a note of originality.

A STAIRWAY GALLERY NEEDN'T BE FAMILY PHOTOS. HERE, THE COLLECTOR HAS GATHERED VINTAGE PHOTOS OF POSED GROUPS, MAKING A WALK UP THE STAIRS INTO A SORT OF JOURNEY THROUGH TIME.

Quick Decorating Idea

One of the most enjoyable and effective transformations of any space is a seasonal display of flowers or foliage. Put out bouquets frequently, letting the arrangements reflect the season as well as your individual style. Try mixing a variety of seasonal blooms like peonies, daisies, roses, verbena, and lilacs; cut the stems at varying lengths to create depth. Or go for a drama—a monochromatic statement featuring a single color. Place flowers in a favorite vase or opt for an untraditional container such as a goblet, bucket, or even a glass canister. Replace the water regularly to keep your fresh-cut bouquets looking their best.

L E F T: The narrow space between these windows offers just the spot for a vintage chair, itself an unexpected delightful spot for a seasonal floral arrangement.

L E F T: In this hallway, the pottery arrangement and flowers counter the formal effect of the wallpaper, suggesting we are heading to a more personal area. The colors in the wallpaper are echoed in the red and white of the pitchers and bench for a unifying effect.

ABOVE: This hallway, with its asymmetry and multiple doorways, offered a true decorating challenge. Among the attractive solutions that transformed it are a pair of benches, one cleverly placed to minimize the sudden widening of the hallway, and three framed pieces, two leaning casually against the walls and one more traditionally placed. A hooked rug with a floral motif marks the passageways to other rooms.

RIGHT: The quickest way to add drama to any doorway? Hang curtains. These diaphanous draperies with pompom trim evoke a bygone era, echoed by the black-and-white travel photographs on the wall.

ABOVE: A windowed hallway with a low wall provides a perfect place for an arrangement of a trunk and a box. The trunk is a hard-working storage piece that is neutral in design and tidy in its use of space.

LEFT: Awkward spaces are found in large rooms as well as small ones. Here, the passage between foyer and living room is enhanced by a dramatic drapery that is both beautiful and practical. In the winter, it helps keep out cold gusts of air from an open door, while year-round its luxuriously rich fabric brings a finishing touch to the European décor.

A B O V E : This steep staircase, with its exposed beams, presents two unusual spaces for decoration. The clear glass jars and milk-pail flower arrangement add a homey touch—and a reason to stop and rest.

TESTING PAINT COLORS

Paint chips are too small to give you a true idea of how colors will behave in your home. Instead, buy some foam core (available at art and craft stores), cut it into 2 x 2-foot sheets, and apply paint to the sheets. Sample-size tins and paint packets are available from companies like Farrow & Ball (farrow-ball.com), Devine Color (devinecolor.com), and Citron Paint & Design (citronpaint.com). When dry, move the sheets around the house to see how colors look in different light, at various times of day, and next to furniture and window treatments.

ABOVE: The warm golden marigold hue in this hallway is repeated below the chair rail in the dining room, and accented with a rustic burnt-sienna wash. This combination of colors and finishes not only connects the two rooms, but balances the interplay of the formal pieces, like the dining chairs and wall sconces, with the more primitive and rough-hewn wooden pieces.

Perfecting Your Palette

Walls and floors are blank canvases for the color and textures that will transform your space. Color on the walls is a most effective creator of mood: bright colors excite, light colors soothe, and combinations can have a variety of effects. Pattern adds another element and may widen or lengthen the room depending on its direction. Similarly, dark colors can make a space seem cozier, while pale tones can visually open a small area. Paintings, photographs, and accoutrements will complete your walls.

While deciding on the color of the walls, you must also consider the floor, which should coordinate with both the color and mood of the wall. Just because it lies beneath your feet doesn't mean this area can be ignored. A properly decorated floor can be a real asset to a small space, making it into a more finished environment. Just close your eyes and imagine cold slate tiles beneath your bare feet, or a plush Persian rug, or scratchy sisal. These materials with their various textures send very different visual messages as well. Nevertheless, you might choose to mix those materials in one room as a very effective way of laying out separate spaces within it. For example, a Persian rug laid atop slate tile will create a warm, cozy conversation zone within a larger, no-nonsense area like a kitchen. Be open to the possibilities of color and texture to create original, surprising, and appealing results.

LEFT: Painting techniques like sponging, combing, and antiquing can alter a room's mood—and you can use the same methods to finish floors, walls, and ceilings. Here, a cottage-y ambience suffuses this small vestibule—the result of mixing colors directly into plaster.

Easy Transformation Tip

BE COLOR-WISE

1. Instead of just one shade, use combinations of similarly hued colors in a room or between rooms to create interest.

2. If you choose to paint each room a different color, make transitions between them by graying down the colors of intervening spaces such as hallways, foyers, and staircases.

3. Create harmonies of color throughout the house by repeating the same hues from room to room—but use them differently. For example, if you choose red paint for the dining room walls, use it on the trim in the living room and as an accent in the fabrics in the kitchen.

4. To make a long, narrow room seem wider, paint the short walls in a dark shade, the long walls in a lighter one.

5. Painting the walls only up to 9 or 12 inches below the ceiling line can lower lofty ceilings and make a space seem cozier. Likewise, painting the wall up to the ceiling line, including the molding, can raise the height of squat rooms.

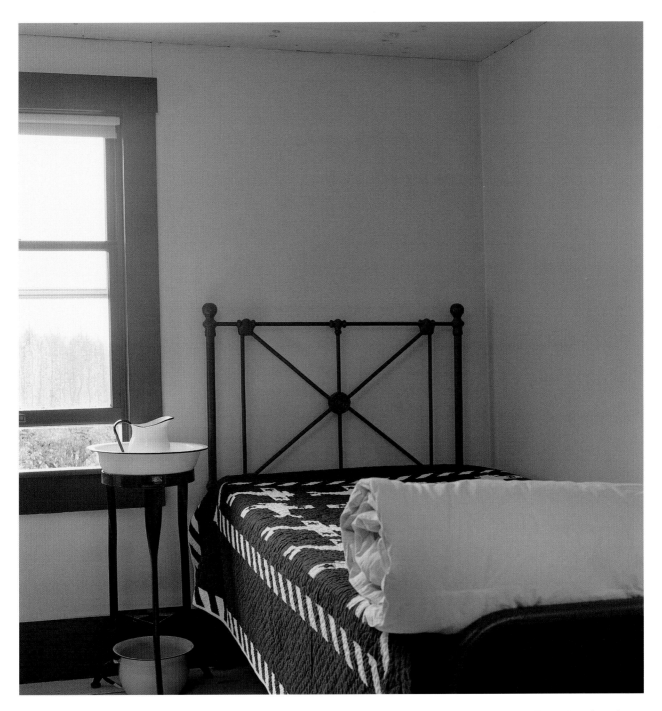

A B O V E : Bold colors can work well on trim when the walls are left a neutral color. Here, the painted trim has become a central theme in a very simple, understated décor.

SEEMINGLY IMPOSSIBLE SPACES
CAN ACTUALLY OFFER EXCELLENT
DISPLAY OPPORTUNITIES.

ABOVE: The type of floor covering you choose can determine your whole response to a room. Easy to care for, all natural, and hypo-allergenic, sea grass is a very popular choice. It adds a wonderful texture and can feel at once elegant yet relaxing.

A B O V E : Beige is not necessarily a boring color scheme when it is carried out in several textures, shades, and patterns. In this dining nook vintage textiles, wicker chairs, and architectural elements—all in soothing shades of beige and white—foster a serene atmosphere.

LEFT: In this foyer the painted floor pattern in chocolate brown and cream balances the door frame's stripped woodwork and the sculptural mahogany banister and newel post of the staircase, all while adding an eccentric charm.

PLACE SOMETHING INTERESTING AT THE TOP AND BOTTOM OF A STAIRCASE.

ABOVE: Decoratively painted floors have a long history in North American and European homes. When restoring this northeastern Connecticut home from 1675 with period details, the owners chose to break up the ubiquitous honey-colored pine with a lively diamond pattern instead of wall-to-wall carpeting. You don't need a period home to have a painted floor, however; a painted trim or an entire floor space painted in single color can transform even the most uninteresting space.

ABOVE: A long, somewhat narrow kitchen with one windowed wall opens up thanks to white paint. Its classic lines and elegant details sparkle in white enamel with white Carrera marble floors. The addition of bold pink peonies in the breakfast nook provides an eye-catching splash of color.

This style of a kitchen but the walls painted bright red with white trim and white floor

AN OFT-NEGLECTED SPOT CAN BENEFIT FROM A SMALL PAINTING.

RIGHT: A small study carries through the home's period charm and antique details while gaining its own individual charm from the painted floor that mimics inlaid marble.

L E F T : Rugs aren't just for the floor. With their bold colors and intricate designs, rugs make excellent wall hangings, even if they're not as colorful as this hooked rug from the 1880s. Not only do they add to the cozy feeling, they also act as effective sound barriers.

R I G H T : Painting the walls and trim in saturated shades of ocher and spruce has lent this room a sense of serendipity and excitement, despite its 200-year-old age. Curtainless windows show off the colorful woodwork and give an unrestrained welcome to the morning sun.

Easy Transformation Tip

HOW TO PAINT A FLOOR

A painted floor—either in a solid color or a pattern—can create a dramatic focal point in a room. Here is how you can achieve this look in your own home.

You will need:
Paint brushes (4-inch width) or mini-rollers
   with low pile
two colors of matte latex paint
a metal yardstick
a pencil
blue painter's tape
Minwax Water-Based Polyurethane
   for Floors

BASE COAT Clean floor. Lay down the paler shade, which will delicately show through later in high-traffic areas. (Note: You may want to start with a primer if your floors are already finished or are dark.)

PATTERN Trace out your lines by hand with a pencil and yardstick. This design is made up of even squares measuring roughly 24 x 24 inches. Don't worry if measuring isn't your strong suit—a slightly tilted grid will lend character.

LAYOUT Mask the exterior of alternating squares with blue painter's tape (i.e., make sure the excess tape is in the box of the second paint color.) Paint squared-off boxes, let dry, then remove the tape. Depending on the degree of coverage, you may need a second coat. After coating with polyurethane, stand back and admire your work of art.

L E F T : Soothing shades of pastel blue, green, and lavender add a note of seaside tranquillity to this bathroom. The checkerboard floor is a creative option that mimics bathroom tile (which would have been more expensive to install), and a painted floor is a nice country touch.

SYMMETRY IS AN EXCELLENT VISUAL TOOL FOR GIVING A SENSE OF
COHERENCE AND ORGANIZATION TO A SMALL ROOM, AS IN THIS BEDROOM
WITH ITS MATCHING BEDS PLACED ON BOTH SIDES OF THE WINDOW, AND
A PAIR OF LAMPS SET ON THE TABLE IN THE MIDDLE.

LEFT: A diminutive black-and-white bathroom undergoes
a transformation from boring to charming by the simple
addition of judicious touches of bright yellow. A decorative
valance trimmed in yellow is a bold choice that gives the
otherwise unremarkable room real personality. Yellow trim
on the sink skirt echoes the valance, and yellow towels
and accessories complete the picture.

ABOVE: A blue-and-yellow palette gives this small
bedroom its sunny charm. Yellow stripes on the walls
create a vivid backdrop for the matching vintage twin
beds, each dressed in similar antique linens in shades
of blue. A soft blue paint links the various pieces of
furniture, while yellow accents spread warmth
throughout the room.

A B O V E : When a room comes with wall-to-wall carpeting that does not entirely suit your style, don't waste time and money replacing it. Cover it with an area rug which will add texture, color, pattern, and style instantly. Laying a rug over carpet can also separate the room into different zones for different activities.

ABOVE: Even the smallest of spaces can be turned into a cozy spot. Such a small space benefits from neutral wall colors, leaving the bed linens to provide some welcome splashes of color. A clever solution to the lack of space was to mount a bedside light on the wall; similarly, a table at the foot of the bed offers a spot for books. Note that the hand-painted table picks up the colors of the quilt and the walls, neatly tying together the room's palette.

ABOVE: Need more light? Add some mirrors. Don't be afraid of using dark, warm colors in a small space: use mirrors to brighten it up and make it seem larger. Displaying them in a jumbled arrangement like this also adds a playful quality. Mirrors can also make a room seem larger.

RIGHT: Calico and homespun fabric arranged alongside dried herbs on an antique drying rack give the perfect touch of authenticity to match the clapboard walls.

Make a Quick Change

Here is a smart way to lighten up a dark wall. A few trips to the flea market (or perhaps your attic) may yield an assortment of vintage frames of different sizes and styles. Paint them with white acrylic or latex, and hang them as a group on a colored wall for a graphic effect. Or, if your walls are white, paint the frames in a bold color.

DON'T BE AFRAID TO CREATE YOUR OWN STILL-LIFES, SUCH AS THIS PAINTERLY ARRANGEMENT. CHANGE THE DETAILS WITH THE SEASON—OR YOUR MOOD.

L E F T : Don't be afraid to use color to support your design statement. Draw upon the colors of your artwork and repeat them in decorative objects throughout the room.

Make a Quick Change

Since they accumulate over time, often collections of family photos are hung together on a wall in frames of all different colors and styles. Reframing this grouping in frames of the same color will unify the entire wall and swiftly update the photos' look from sentimental to sensational—a simple but dramatic change.

Easy Transformation Tip

HOW TO FRAME A PICTURE

Create a custom-look frame for your family photos by choosing museum-quality materials, including mat board and photo corners. Ready-to-use mats and frames can often be found for standard-size photos, while images or frames of irregular sizes or shapes will need custom-cut mats, which can be ordered at frame shops (bring the photo with you for best fit). Cut-to-size glass and Plexiglas with UV protection is easily obtained at industrial glass suppliers (check your phone book for nearby locations). Gather your materials—a bottom mat, top mat with cut-out window, glass, frame, and photo corners—onto a clean surface in a well-lit area.

1. Align the photograph on the bottom mat and attach with photo corners.

2. Place the window mat over the photo.

3. Pick up the bottom mat, photograph, and top mat and carefully turn all three over. Set top mat against glass in frame.

4. Seal the frame; hang or display the finished piece away from direct sunlight.

RIGHT: If you love the architectural details of Early American homes, but prefer low-maintenance living, use your walls as a gallery for an eclectic assortment of architectural pieces. Don't go carving up houses yourself, though, because architectural salvage requires professional know-how. Instead, go hunting for the impressive pieces that are readily available at antique stores and flea markets.

LEFT: Consider papering just one wall in a cheerful, cottage-inspired style. Another option: Create stripes with two colors of paint. Choose two contrasting shades, or go tone-on-tone (a lighter and darker shade from the same family) for a soothing effect.

ABOVE: When your desk faces a blank wall, inspiration can be difficult to find. Instead of cluttering that space with memos and reminders that would detract from the room's décor, make an inspiring collage from magazine clippings, fabric swatches, and art you admire. It will add pizzazz to your creative corner.

RIGHT: The kitchen is the perfect space for a bit of whimsy. This rustic coatrack holds outdoor gear and vintage fishing nets from Maine (giving you an idea of how those Sunday hours are spent), which adds a hint of country charm without being precious.

Decorating Idea

When hanging a large grouping of pictures, first lay them out on the floor to get a sense of how the images relate to one other. In particular, if the frames are different shapes or sizes, it is better to have a sense of how their proportions relate before driving in the first nail. Try to keep the perimeter of the collection square, and pictures more or less at eye level. If the grouping is hanging in a stairwell, keep the bottom and top of the group at the same height relative to the risers.

ABOVE: The space above the mantel is an ideal spot to express yourself. Many people opt for a large piece of art—one bold statement. A grouping of many small objects in several formats, as shown in this silhouette arrangement, can be just as effective.

ABOVE: This romantic bud vase is a neat way to add some natural beauty to any room. Simply tie a ribbon around the neck of a bottle and hang it from a nail anywhere it looks best. The only care it will require is freshening the flowers.

ABOVE: This wall uses a collection of found objects to create an entertaining focal point for this living room. On it, a grouping of small-scale mirrors is accompanied by an ornamental pediment, and a shelf trimmed in antique lace holds a shell-covered birdhouse and a metal rowboat from the 1930s.

LEFT: One small framed piece of art can get lost on a large wall. Covering a wall with small, matching artworks makes a bold statement. The striped wallpaper behind these botanical drawings provides a lively background.

Creating Nooks and Crannies in Any Room

When you're accustomed to decorating small spaces, it is easy to be intimidated by a large room. But it is important to take advantage of all the spatial opportunities any room offers. The trick is to develop the same dramatic interest you've created in a cozy corner but on a larger scale. Break up the room into informal zones, using rugs over wooden flooring, painting architectural features in different colors, or turning a piece of furniture in another direction. An overstuffed armchair; a corner table draped with an oversize cloth; a long, sloping chaise lounge—one of these might be just the remedy for what ails your space. Be sure to use all the tricks of the trade; just as we have done in the rooms that follow. Remember that lighting, color, textures, wall hangings, and decorative objects are the vocabulary you are using to describe your design scheme and to welcome yourself and your guests into each room. It may surprise you how much one of these small changes can enhance the joy and relaxation you will experience in your home.

LEFT: When designing your own home from the ground up, you can create truly customized cozy spots. This alcove surrounded by cedar wainscoting is for nesting beneath the window at the top of the stairs. As a special area for children, it can be improved only by the addition of a blanket over the opening to create a secret fort.

ABOVE: A loving renovation of this century-old home, part of New York's Mills Mansion State Historic Site, has created modern, flexible spaces. Here, the mismatched chairs of the dining room make it feel like a cozy nook. The kitchen, visible through the doorway to the left, has a charming side table of its own with a table lamp instead of an overhead light that creates a more intimate feel.

KEEP THE TOP OF A
CUPBOARD NEAT BY
STASHING ITEMS IN
ATTRACTIVE BASKETS
OR OTHER CONTAINERS.

RIGHT: One sure-fire way to make a corner more cozy is to add a table. This arrangement creates a small conversation area or a place to sit and peruse a book.

RIGHT: Humor reveals your personality and charms visitors. While elegant, this dining room cleverly incorporates unexpected elements. Folding French garden chairs pull up to a Swedish dining table. Ivy embellishes the Italian tole chandelier and adjustable candelabra found at a Paris flea market. A 1920s hooked rug sets off the table, and continues the garden theme.

DRAMATIC DRAPERIES NOT ONLY FRAME A WINDOW, THEY ALSO BRING A SENSE OF WARMTH AND INTIMACY TO A SPACE.

LEFT: An elegant table setting enlivens this corner. The placement of a French pastoral scene, framed with a mirror beneath it so that it reflects light from the candelabra, heightens the romantic effect.

ABOVE: This wraparound shelf is a clever way to utilize space below a window and above a radiator and creates a natural reading alcove for two in a sunny, open room.

IF PRIVACY IS NOT AN ISSUE, LEAVING WINDOWS UNCOVERED CAN HAVE THE EFFECT OF BLURRING THE BOUNDARIES BETWEEN OUTDOORS AND IN, CREATING A "GARDEN ROOM" INSIDE.

L E F T : Corner tables create surfaces for displaying objects, and they can add needed color and texture to a room. The toasty tartan wool tablecloth on this table warms up the room's otherwise cool ambience and adds dimension to the room with its diagonal lines.

Make a Quick Change

CREATE VINTAGE-STYLE LINENS

Whether you have permanent stains on a much-loved tablecloth, or are just drawn to the nostalgic look of aged textiles, here's an easy project to try with any cotton or linen fabrics, patterned or plain.

BOIL a pot of water and add regular tea bags (from four bags for two napkins to 20 bags for a small tablecloth; control the degree of staining by varying steeping times).

SOAK FABRIC in the pot from 15 minutes to overnight; remember that the stain appears darker when wet, but will lighten quite a bit when dry.

RINSE FABRIC thoroughly in cold water with a tablespoon of white vinegar to set.

DRY FABRIC in a clothes dryer and clean the dryer after use.

A B O V E : Overstuffed, comfy furniture instantly makes a room feel relaxing. As if this display of chairs in pink-and-white toile and cottage roses weren't welcoming enough, the seersucker chaise lounge in the corner rounds out the trio magnificently. The use of café curtains at the window, as opposed to traditional drapes, completes the room's informal air.

L E F T : An efficient use of space, the breakfast nook is a classic choice for small kitchens. Here, the pastoral color scheme really makes it stand out. The country-style furniture, chandelier, and Canton china and willowware platters on the wall lend a homey aspect.

ABOVE : A new bay window in a formerly dark kitchen offers bright light and space for a dining alcove in a kitchen too small for a full-size table and chairs. The chintz on the pillows picks up the colors in the patterned plates above, and is further accented by the lampshade.

RIGHT : A bay window is a perfect location for a dining nook, and this one has used every inch of space to convey a comfortable country setting. A shelf above the window displays a small collection of pottery with clean lines. The wrought-iron table adds a delicate touch, and the wicker club chairs invite relaxation.

LEFT: Large, modern spaces can still be warm and welcoming. Some of the touches that make this sleek space more intimate include painting the wall across from the kitchen counter a warm red, creating an inviting area for guests to relax by the fire, and using comfortable chairs to soften the look. For a cook who enjoys an audience, this setup couldn't be better.

ABOVE: Placement of furniture can make a huge difference in how a room feels. Here, nestling the bed into a corner ensures a sense of snug security—while the window keeps guests from feeling closed in.

RIGHT: This Victorian fainting couch, upholstered in cotton with crewel florets, has made the corner a natural spot for reflection in a room of serene pastels. Its placement, angled toward the center of the room, allows its beautiful lines to be appreciated from both sides.

A VINTAGE FRENCH BEDSTEAD DRAPED IN LAYERS OF LUXURIOUS LINENS IS TOO INVITING TO RESIST. QUILTS LAYERED IN A BASKET ADD TO THE ROOM'S COTTAGE-LIKE COMFORT.

LEFT: A bedroom with an alcove, an otherwise awkward "L" shape, lends itself to this curtain treatment to set up a private dressing room. Romance and femininity are inherent in the design, but emphasized by the long, full drapes, pink-striped wallpaper, and accoutrements like the hot pink tulle-skirted gown.

ABOVE: A small area rug in the center of three chairs makes an effective conversation spot for small gatherings. With their strong bearing but tattered paint jobs, these chairs look like old friends gathered together.

a dressing room

←

LEFT: In a busy kitchen with all corners filled by appliances, it can be difficult to set aside space. Laying down a petite rag rug can section off an area visually so you can add a small table and chairs without them appearing awkward.

TUCKING A ROW OF FRAMED PIECES BENEATH THE PLATE RAIL LOWERS THE HEIGHT OF THE ROOM'S CEILING, MAKING A LARGE SPACE A LITTLE MORE INTIMATE.

ABOVE: This corner was made for reading and relaxing. The botanical print on the chair echoes the prints on the wall, allowing the chair to blend into its surroundings like a garden bench. The textured rug is reminiscent of a garden trellis.

LEFT: This sun porch will bring spring to life in the midst of winter. Floral pillows made from sample yardage add an inviting touch to a bent-willow love seat and a green rocker, a nineteenth-century Pennsylvania piece. Brightly striped curtains add a summer cabana feeling to the room, and they can completely cover the windows when the day is not as sunny as they are.

ABOVE: A massive, overstuffed club chair attired in faded country florals reigns over this corner, nearly commanding relaxation by its presence. The antique dressing-room screen painted with a Monet-inspired scene serves as an unexpected backdrop.

L E F T : In a small space, furniture placement is key— don't be afraid to partially block windows to make a room work. Here, a vintage iron bed is tucked between two windows, but its open headboard and low footboard let the light shine in.

A HOOK-AND-SHELF COMBINATION CAN HOLD A VARIETY OF ITEMS YET STILL LOOK CHARMING BECAUSE OF ITS RUSTIC ORIGINS.

R I G H T : Centered in front of a window, the bed forms the focal point of this room. The window treatment makes it work: sheer panels let in light while offering privacy, and heavier drapes for nighttime keep it warm and cozy.

R I G H T : Textiles are excellent tools for creating cozy spaces. The colors in this room are soft and warm, just right for a guest bedroom with a private entrance. Inside, hand-crocheted and embroidered curtains share the stage with graphic quilts and woven cotton rugs. The mix of textures keeps it interesting.

ABOVE: This open-air porch, added onto the brick façade as an afterthought, brings the outdoors inside with a hanging wicker swing, fern-stenciled flooring, and loads of plants. Who wouldn't want to relax here on a warm summer's day?

ABOVE: This porch room has become a retreat. The outdoor furniture brought indoors, layers of cotton ticking fabric, and bucket of hydrangeas add up to a romantic retreat.

Working Spaces

Too often we leave the rooms we work in unadorned, as though we oppose mixing business with pleasure. Yet no matter how small the area, a splash of color, a personal touch, or a hint of humor can work wonders for our mood as we do the laundry, pay the bills, or put the mop away.

A new potential problem for the home decorator is that with the growing trend of working from home, poorly adapted work spaces are taking over much-needed living space and filling formerly attractive rooms with ugly office equipment.

It is important to set aside space for each activity in the home. Placing even a small desk in one corner, adding hidden storage throughout the room, or otherwise camouflaging work tools will allow several functions to take place at different hours of the day without compromising the visual appeal and comfort factor of a room. It is also important to create separation between work and home life. The solutions presented here are wide-ranging and practical, but they are far from the only options. Let them get you started thinking about what will work best in your home.

L E F T : Even doing laundry can be fun if you outfit your space creatively. Here, an antique dollhouse doubles as a cabinet, holding detergents and sundries, while a doll's bed outfitted with wheels serves as a laundry cart.

ABOVE: A home office should be both efficient and comfortable. If space is available, a four-drawer c. 1860 Pennsylvania work table like this one will get the job done. It is also important to surround yourself with things you love. The redware plates, homespun feed sacks, and wooden candlepins help make the room an enjoyable place to spend time.

WALLS ARE OFTEN OVERLOOKED STORAGE AREAS. THINK ABOUT ITEMS ON YOUR DESK THAT COULD JUST AS EASILY BE KEPT ABOVE IT, ON SHELVES, PEG RAILS, OR PEG BOARD.

LEFT: This stationer's card-display rack, abandoned by its original owner, takes on a second life above this desk. Racks can hold bills to be paid, party invitations, tickets to a play, vacation postcards, important business cards, and more, all organized, and displayed to remind you what to do next.

Make a Quick Change

A little paint and a cotton dish towel is all it takes to turn an ugly side chair into an appealing desk chair.

TOOLS Sandpaper, paintbrushes, alkyd primer, alkyd interior paint (satin or semi-gloss finish wears best), staple gun, 1-inch-thick foam rubber cut same size as seat, fabric (8 inches larger than seat), long pins, double-sided tape, adhesive tape, scissors.

PAINT Remove seat from chair carefully. Sand chair. Wipe clean. Apply one coat of primer; let dry. Apply one to two coats of interior paint; let dry.

UPHOLSTER Discard old foam pad; secure new foam to seat with double-sided tape.

Lay seat on a clean surface, foam side up. Pin fabric to foam top (align patterned fabrics carefully). Flip seat over. Fold fabric (top first, then bottom) over seat edges, pulling smooth but not too tight. Tape to seat bottom as needed, 1 inch from edge, 1 to 1½ inches apart (closer around curves). Staple fabric over edges. Remove pins from seat top; refasten seat to chair.

TIPS Wrapping the seat first in medium-weight muslin serves as practice and results in a smoother fabric fit. Another trick is to clip the fabric at inner curves and staple pleats around outer curves. If all else fails, recruit an assistant to fold and hold the fabric in place while you staple.

RIGHT: A bedroom work space matches the room's décor with a built-in shelf desk fitted with ornate corbels to blend with the romantic atmosphere. All the pencils, sticky notes, and other clutter are contained in scalloped oval boxes.

Easy Transformation Tip

HOME OFFICE ESSENTIALS

1. KEEP IT BASIC Simple furniture styles will fit in with any décor. Personalize the space with chair cushions, throw pillows, and customized lampshades that won't cost much to replace as your tastes change.

2. CURB THE CLUTTER A cluttered desk makes for a disorganized mind. Stackable boxes corral desktop essentials.

3. CLEAR THE DECK A wall lamp, bulletin board, and keyboard tray free up the desktop and help make the most of any space.

4. INVITE MORE LIGHT Positioning the desk near a source of natural light will help you whistle while you work. A window shade will cut the glare if necessary.

LEFT: A simple sawhorse table and schoolhouse chair painted in calming colors leave plenty of room for fun. Bright colors, like this jolt of chartreuse, chase away institutional drab from file cabinets, and kitschy posters and plaques add to the lively atmosphere.

RIGHT: Just because it's a storage closet doesn't mean it should be ugly or disorganized. A vintage homemade hanging organizer holds cleaning supplies neatly and honors the work of the person who once made it.

LEFT: As an alternative to attempting to make a small kitchen seem larger, maximize the feeling of intimacy instead. This kitchen, though narrow, benefits from lots of natural light in the daytime, so it doesn't feel cramped. Downlights in the ceiling and a slender lamp provide illumination at night. An interior window opens up the space above the counter. The overall effect: small but cozy.

ABOVE: A built-in counter provides side-by-side space—and all the necessary Internet connections—for two people to tackle work or manage household finances. Built-ins are wonderful space savers because they adapt to your space better than ready-made furniture.

Easy Transformation Tip

BULLETIN BOARDS

Cork bulletin boards aren't very attractive. To make a board that suits your style, cut a mat board to fit the frame of your choice. Cut additional strips of mat board to the same width as the frame. Then, for a decorative look, glue seamstress's tape or ribbon to the top edge of each strip. Working from top to bottom, create "pockets" by gluing the bottom edge of the strips to the board with a hot glue gun. Overlap strips as you go. Fit the mat into the frame, and secure it to the back of the frame with hot glue or a few brads.

L E F T : A dining area can do double duty as a place to store items that don't fit elsewhere—if you make it look good. Start with custom-built shelving, open if (as here) you plan to store something visually appealing. These shelves are stacked with china and pewter that is too beautiful to be hidden. This frees up cupboard space in the kitchen for less attractive items.

LEFT: Turnabout is fair play—
if shelves can hold china, cupboards can hold books. This mid-
nineteenth-century New England
step-back cupboard now houses
cookbooks in a breakfast room,
and the artful display of everyday
silverware in vintage trophy cups
has freed another drawer.

RIGHT: Another bookcase would have closed in the space and
blocked light from the window, but this late nineteenth-century folding
ladder just fills the bill. It adds storage while displaying design books,
turn-of-the-century French maple reticulated glove hands, and plaster
casts of European composers.

L E F T : Storage crates with trays are very handy for keeping your things neat and organized, but unless your style is very modern, you don't want them to be seen. You can hide them in plain sight— and save space—by covering them with a decorative cloth and using them as side tables.

R I G H T : Labels on containers can illustrate where items go and help advance the vocabularies of young readers. When organizing a child's space, fun is an important element. Bright colors attract young eyes, and the vintage alphabet letters keep adult interest.

ABOVE: An office doesn't have to look high-tech to be efficient. This former sleeping porch with a wicker desk and laptop computer actually serves as headquarters to a home-based beauty-product business selling all-natural skin-care formulas to over 3,000 customers. A cottage-style washstand does double duty as file cabinet and plant stand. The attractive surroundings make this home office a pleasant place to spend time.

LEFT: When you think you have no room for a home office, take another look at that closet. Removing the doors, hanging long curtains, and painting the interior a bright yellow created this diminutive but efficient home office. It provides a separate work space that can be hidden with a flick of the wrist.

Photography Credits

Index